BIBLE STORIES

PUBLICATIONS INTERNATIONAL, LTD.

BIBLE STORIES

TABLE OF CONTENTS

God's Creation

Retold by Lora Kalkman   *Illustrated by Beatriz Vidal*

In the beginning, God created the heavens and the earth.

At first, the earth was dark. So God created light.

"Let there be light," God said. Then light appeared. God created light and darkness on the first day.

On the second day, God separated the blue waters of the earth from the blue skies above.

On the third day, God created land. He separated the dry land from the water. God also made winding rivers and babbling streams. He made small ponds and big lakes, too.

On the land, God made tiny hills and giant mountains. When God finished, he looked at the earth he had made. "This is good," God said.

Then God filled the earth with grasses, plants, and trees. He created all of the beautiful flowers. God also made every kind of tree.

On the fourth day, God created the sun, the moon, and the stars. He made the golden sun and placed it in the sky. He made the sun shine during the day to make the earth bright.

God also created the moon. He placed the moon in the sky to shine at night. Then God created millions of twinkling stars. He placed each one in the heavens above the earth.

When God had finished, he looked at his creation. "This is good," he said again.

On the fifth day, God created all creatures in the sea and all birds in the sky.

First God said, "Let the waters teem with swarms of living creatures."

Then, in the waters, God placed millions of fish. He made fish of all shapes and sizes. He made tiny orange goldfish and large spotted trout. He made giant black and white whales. God made starfish and sea horses and jellyfish, too. He also made dolphins and eels.

Then God said, "Let birds fly above the earth."

God created every kind of bird. He made little birds and big birds. He made bluebirds, red cardinals, and seagulls. God made giant eagles and owls that hoot.

God blessed all of the birds and all the creatures in the sea that he had made.

On the sixth day, God created all the other living creatures.

First, he made all of the animals of the earth. He made elephants and lions and placed them in the jungles. God made cows, sheep, and goats to graze in the fields. He made deer, squirrels, and rabbits and placed them in forests. God made dogs and cats and horses, too.

God also made all of the bugs and insects of the earth. He made buzzing bees. He made spiders that spin webs. God made every animal on the earth.

Then God created man. He named the man Adam and the woman Eve. God saw all that he had made and it was very good.

On the seventh day, God rested. God blessed the seventh day, which is now called Sunday. It is a day to remember God's wonderful creation.

Adam and Eve

Retold by Lora Kalkman   *Illustrated by Richard Bernal*

After God created the earth, God created man in his own image. The man was named Adam.

God created a glorious garden where Adam lived. It was called the Garden of Eden. God planted beautiful flowers and tall trees. He filled the garden with fruits and vegetables.

Adam enjoyed his lovely home. He took care of the plants and animals. Still, God could see that Adam was lonely.

God decided to make a partner for Adam. When Adam was asleep, God took one of his ribs. Then he made a woman. The woman was named Eve.

God only asked Adam and Eve to follow one rule. In the middle of the garden stood a very large tree filled with big red fruit.

"This tree," God told them, "is called the tree of the knowledge of good and evil. You may eat from any tree in the garden except this one."

One day while Eve was out on a walk, she noticed all of the big red fruit dangling from the branches of the tree of the knowledge of good and evil.

The red fruit did look
delicious, but Eve remembered
God's rule. They could eat from any tree
but that one.

While Adam was picking apples from a smaller tree
nearby, a long snake approached Eve. The snake knew about God's rule,
but the snake was very sneaky and bad. He wanted to tempt Eve into
disobeying God.

"Eve," the sly snake hissed, "why don't you pick some apples from that
big tree over there? They are bigger and sweeter."

The snake pointed to the forbidden tree. Eve knew God did not want
her to eat the fruit.

Eve thought the fruit on the forbidden tree did look delicious.
She felt it would be a shame if the fruit went to waste. Still, she
remembered God's rule.

Then the snake slithered closer and whispered in Eve's
ear. "If you eat from that tree, you will become
wise," he said slyly. "You will become
smart like God. That is why God
doesn't want you to eat from
the tree. He is afraid you
will become as smart as
he is."

Eve wanted to become
as smart as God.

Foolishly, Eve walked over and picked
two pieces of fruit from the forbidden tree. Eve
took a bite of the fruit. Then she handed a piece to
Adam. He also took a bite of the
forbidden fruit.

God was watching them. He became
very sad when Adam and Eve broke his only
rule. God loved Adam and Eve, but now he had to
punish them.

God went to the garden to find Adam and Eve.

"Where are you?" God called.

"We are hiding," Adam said. "We are
embarrassed because we are not wearing
any clothes."

"Then you must have eaten from the
tree of the knowledge of good and evil,"
God said.

"Yes," Adam said. "Eve offered me a piece of
fruit from the forbidden tree, and I ate it." Adam
felt ashamed.

God turned to Eve. "Is this true?"

"Yes," Eve replied. "The snake tricked me.
He said I would be smart and wise if I ate
the fruit from the tree, so I did. I knew
I was not supposed to."

Then God punished them for breaking his rule. He forced the snake to slither on the ground. He made the snake an enemy to men and women.

"The snake will now be able to bite and poison you," God told Adam and Eve. "Men and women will now step on you," he said to the snake.

Then God told Adam and Eve they would have to leave the Garden of Eden. No longer would they enjoy their beautiful home that he had made for them.

"I was happy to give you everything, but you broke my only rule," God told them. "Now you will have to plant your own garden and grow your own food. You will have to work hard to build a new home that protects you from the rain and cold."

God watched with sorrow as Adam and Eve left his garden. God knew life would be difficult for Adam and Eve. This made God sad. Even though Adam and Eve had disobeyed him, he still loved them.

After Adam and Eve left, God asked angels to guard the Garden of Eden. Sadly, because Adam and Eve had broken God's only rule, they were never allowed to return to the garden ever again.

Noah's Ark

Retold by Leslie Lindecker   Illustrated by Mike Jaroszko

Many years after God had created the earth, most of the people had turned away from him. This made God sad. He wanted to wash the earth clean and make it good once again.

One man still obeyed God. His name was Noah. "I have a special plan for you and your family," God said. "I am going to cause a flood to wash the earth clean of all the evil and wickedness. You and your family have found favor with me. I will spare your lives."

Noah listened carefully to everything God told him. "You must build an ark," God said. "It should be made of gopher wood. You must seal the wood with tree sap inside and out. The sap will keep the water out. Put a window near the top of the ark and a large door opening onto the lower three floors.

"When the time comes, I will send two of every kind of animal on earth to you. They will come in pairs, one male and one female, and you will shelter them in the ark. I will send the birds of the sky and everything that walks and crawls on the ground. You and your family must gather food for yourselves and for all of the animals and store it on the ark."

God continued, "When you see the rain begin, gather your family onto the ark with all of the animals. Then close the doors."

Noah trusted God. He told his family what God had said. The family prayed together. The next day, Noah and his sons began to build the ark.

Noah's neighbors came by to see what was going on. "Why are you building such a big boat?" his neighbors wanted to know.

Noah told them what God had said about washing the earth clean of all the wickedness and evil. His neighbors laughed and turned away, shaking their heads at Noah's foolishness.

Noah and his sons continued to work hard on the ark. They built the huge boat and coated it with tree sap inside and out so water would not leak in. They put a small window near the top and a large door opening onto the bottom three floors.

When Noah and his sons finished the ark they started gathering food for their family and all of the animals. Then an amazing thing happened.

From all directions animals began to come to the ark. They came in pairs, one male and one female. Tiny mice and ladybugs walked to the ark. Tall giraffes and round elephants also came to the ark. Noah watched as the smallest hummingbirds and the mightiest eagles flew to the ark. The lions roared, the owls hooted, and the snakes slithered. All of the animals came in peace to the ark.

Noah and his family put all of the animals into the rooms in the ark. They tried to make them as comfortable as they could.

A week later it started to rain. The skies grew dark and the clouds began to roll and build. Lightning flashed and thunder boomed. Noah and his family were safe and dry inside the ark. They could not hear anything outside the ark except the storm. They took care of each other and of all the animals on the ark. God protected everyone and everything on the ark from the storm.

It rained for forty days and forty nights. All the earth was flooded. God washed away all the evil and wickedness. Noah and his family were the only people who survived the flood. The animals on the ark were also safe.

Noah and his wife kept busy feeding all the birds. The wives of his sons kept very busy feeding all the animals. Noah's sons kept very, very busy cleaning up after all the birds and the animals.

God kept peace among all of the animals and the birds who were all used to roaming and flying free across the earth. They ate fruits and grains right from the hands of Noah and his family. Because Noah's family trusted God, they were not afraid of any of the animals. Even the growling tigers and snapping crocodiles were calm and peaceful.

The rain stopped after forty days and forty nights. The ark bobbed about on the floodwater for 150 more days. God sent a great wind to make the water go down. Then the ark came to rest on the top of a mountain.

Noah felt the ark settle on solid ground. He went to the top of the ark and looked out the window. But he could only see water. Noah knew they could not yet leave the ark.

Later, Noah looked out the window again. This time he saw mountaintops above the water.

Then Noah sent out a dove. The dove flew about looking for land. When she did not find land, she returned to the ark and landed on Noah's hand.

Noah waited a week and sent the dove out again to look for dry land. She returned with a sprig from an olive tree. Noah knew that there was dry land. He waited one more week and sent the dove out once again.

This time she did not return. Noah knew the dove had finally found a place to live on dry land.

God spoke to Noah. "Leave the ark. Take your family with you. Bring out all the animals. The earth has been cleaned and is now yours to care for." Noah and his wife left the ark. His sons, Shem, Ham, and Japheth, and their wives left the ark. The birds flew from the ark and the animals walked, slithered, crawled, hopped, and ran from the ark into the newly cleaned world.

Noah built a special altar and praised God for taking care of them. God was pleased with Noah and his family.

God told Noah, "I will never again curse the earth because of man's wicked heart. I will never again destroy everything to wash the earth clean as I have done this time. Planting time and harvest time, cold and heat, summer and winter, and day and night shall not end as long as the earth remains."

God blessed Noah and
his family. "I will put my
promise to you in the sky,"
God said to Noah. Then
God painted a rainbow
across the sky.

"This is my sign. I will
never again cover the whole
earth with water. Whenever
you, your children, or your
children's children see my
rainbow in the sky, it will
be a beautiful reminder of
my promise."

Noah and his family lived
very long and happy lives.
They all had many children,
grandchildren, and even
great-grandchildren. They all
loved God and remembered his
promise when they saw his rainbow
after a thunderstorm.

The animals and birds spread throughout the
world and had chicks and pups and kittens and foals. And when
they think no one is watching, they too are looking to the sky for God's promise in
his rainbow.

Joseph's Coat

Retold by Lisa Harkrader   *Illustrated by Stacey Schuett*

Joseph held up the coat his father, Jacob, had given him. "I can't believe you had this made just for me," Joseph said.

"I believe it," his brother Judah muttered.

Joseph's ten older brothers watched as he put on the coat. It was finely woven and made of so many colors it looked as if a rainbow had burst onto it. It was the most beautiful coat they had ever seen.

The brothers thought Joseph was their father's favorite son.

"We have work to do," muttered Judah.

The brothers went back into the fields to work. They left Joseph and their father together to admire the beautiful new coat.

One night not long afterward, Joseph had a strange dream. In this dream, Joseph and his brothers were working in their father's field. They were cutting wheat and tying it into bundles. Suddenly, Joseph's bundle of wheat stood up tall and straight. His brothers' bundles of wheat bowed down low to Joseph's bundle.

"What do you think it means?" Joseph asked.

"It means you think too much of yourself," said Judah. "Do you really think we would all bow down to you?"

The next night, Joseph had another dream. In this one the sun, the moon, and eleven stars all bowed down to him.

When Joseph woke up, he ran to tell his whole family about his dream.

"What does it means?" Joseph asked.

This time even Joseph's father was shocked by the dream. But old Jacob did not forget about Joseph's dream. Jacob wondered if someday Joseph's dream would come true.

One day, when Joseph's older brothers were tending their father's flock, Jacob sent Joseph to find them. When Joseph reached his brothers they grabbed him, tore off his many-colored coat, and threw him into an empty well. Later, they sold him to a trade caravan.

Joseph's brothers tore the many-colored coat to shreds. They dipped it in goat's blood and gave it to their father.

Jacob took the blood-stained coat. "No!" he cried. "My son! Joseph is dead."

But Joseph was not dead. The traders sold Joseph to Pharaoh's officials. Pharaoh was the ruler of Egypt.

The officials put Joseph in charge of Pharaoh's jail. The prisoners trusted Joseph and began telling him their dreams.

Joseph explained the dreams, and everything he told them came true. Soon Pharaoh began having strange dreams. The officials brought Joseph to Pharaoh. Pharaoh told Joseph about his dreams.

"In one dream," said Pharaoh, "seven fat cows came up from the river and grazed in the thick grass. Then seven skinny cows came up and swallowed the fat cows. In another dream, seven plump ears of corn sprouted on a cornstalk. Then seven withered ears of corn sprouted and swallowed the good corn."

"The seven fat cows and seven plump ears of corn stand for seven years of good harvests," Joseph explained. "The seven skinny cows and seven withered ears of corn stand for seven years of bad harvests. For the next seven years, Egypt will have more food than the people can eat. Then the rain will stop. For the next seven years Egypt will not grow enough food to feed the people."

Joseph told Pharaoh to store extra grain during the seven good years. During the seven bad years, the people would have enough to eat.

Pharaoh appointed Joseph to oversee the harvests. Joseph became the highest official in all of Egypt. The only person more powerful than Joseph was Pharaoh.

For seven years the land of Egypt had good crops and Joseph stored grain. At the end of seven years all the crops died. But Joseph had stored enough food.

In the land of Canaan, where Joseph's family lived, the people had not stored grain. They were hungry. Jacob heard about the grain in Egypt. He gathered his ten oldest sons and gave them sacks of silver.

Jacob sent his sons to Egypt to buy grain. The brothers were brought before Joseph. Joseph recognized his brothers at once. But he decided not to tell them who he was.

"Are you your father's only sons?" Joseph asked.

"There are two more," Reuben said. "Joseph is gone. Benjamin stayed home."

"I'll sell you the grain you need, but you must bring Benjamin back to me," said Joseph. "I'll keep your brother Simeon here in Egypt."

Joseph told his assistant to fill his brothers' sacks with grain. Then he ordered them to secretly put his brothers' silver back into the sacks before tying them shut.

When Joseph's brothers returned to Canaan, they were surprised to find the silver in their sacks. Their father was furious that they had left Simeon behind.

"But if we take Benjamin to meet Pharaoh's high official," Reuben explained, "he'll let Simeon go."

"Joseph is gone and now Simeon is lost, too," Jacob cried. "I won't risk Benjamin's life. Pharaoh's official must think you stole that silver from him."

Soon, though, Jacob's family needed more food. Jacob had to send his sons to Egypt again.

"Pay for the grain you took last time," he said. "Then buy another load of grain to bring home."

The brothers set off for Egypt. This time Benjamin went with them.

Joseph was happy to see his brothers again. Joseph told his assistant to fill their bags with grain and to secretly place his favorite cup in Benjamin's bag.

Joseph's brothers had not gone far when Joseph's assistant stopped them. He searched their bags and found Joseph's cup in Benjamin's sack of grain.

Joseph stood before them. "You are free to go, but Benjamin stays here."

"No," cried Reuben. "We're brothers. If Benjamin stays, we all stay."

Joseph was happy to hear that his brothers would not abandon Benjamin. "I'm your brother, too. I am Joseph." Joseph's brothers could not believe their eyes. Joseph sent for his father and for his brothers' families. Pharaoh gave them all land to live on.

"There was a reason my brothers sold me," said Joseph. "God wanted me in Egypt. He wanted me to save the Egyptian people and my family."

Miriam and Moses

Retold by Sarah Toast   *Illustrated by Kathy Mitchell*

Jochebed came into the house after a day of hard work in the fields. Her daughter, Miriam, poured her a glass of sweetened water. Jochebed's young son, Aaron, played at her feet. Miriam could tell that something was troubling her mother.

"I have dreadful news," said Jochebed. "It is not enough that Pharaoh has turned us into slaves and made our days miserable. Though we are treated harshly, we continue to grow in size and strength, so Pharaoh is afraid of us—afraid that we will rise up against him or that we will help an enemy that tries to conquer him."

"But how could Pharaoh treat us any more harshly?" Miriam asked her mother.

"There is worse to come, my child," said her mother. "Pharaoh has ordered the Israelite nurses to kill all baby boys born to us."

"That's dreadful, Mother!" Miriam exclaimed. "What if our new baby is a boy?"

"God will help us," Jochebed said.

As the weeks passed, Jochebed brought news from the field that all the new Israelite baby boys were well after all. "The nurses refuse to do as Pharaoh ordered. Perhaps we do not need to worry so!"

Later, Miriam went to the well where the women drew water for their households and exchanged news. A kind woman helped Miriam pull up the heavy pail from the well. The woman leaned close to Miriam and quietly told her something. When Miriam got home, she sadly told her mother what the woman at the well had said.

"Pharaoh is angry that his orders weren't obeyed," Miriam told her. "Now he has ordered all Egyptians to throw every Israelite baby boy into the Nile."

A few days later, Jochebed called Miriam to her side.

"Miriam," said Jochebed. "It is time to get the nurse to help me with the new baby. But be careful not to let anyone else know."

Soon Miriam was back with the nurse. Miriam left the nurse with her mother and took Aaron down to the river.

"I'll show you how to make a little raft of woven reeds to float on the Nile," said Miriam to Aaron. Miriam took care of Aaron at the river all afternoon.

When Miriam brought Aaron back home at dinnertime, there was a new baby in the house.

"Meet your new baby brother," said Jochebed happily.

"He is a such a beautiful baby!" said Miriam as she kissed his forehead.

"We must hide him from sight," said Jochebed.

"I'll help you," Miriam said.

For three long months, the family took care of the little baby boy without the Egyptians knowing about him.

When the Egyptians made their sweeping searches of Israelite homes and yards, Jochebed hid her little baby in a basket.

One day, Miriam went to the river's edge to gather reeds to make baskets. Suddenly, Pharaoh's beautiful daughter came to the river with her servants.

"I have seen the princess here before," thought Miriam. "I must remember what days she comes to the river to bathe."

One morning, Jochebed said, "I don't think we can hide the baby much longer."

"Do not worry," Miriam said. "I have a plan."

Miriam helped her mother make a special basket in the shape of a little boat. Before full light, Miriam and her mother quietly took the baby in the basket to the place by the riverbed where Pharaoh's daughter bathed. There the Israelite mother and daughter set the basket in the thick reeds. The basket bobbed gently on the water, lulling the baby to sleep. Jochebed went back home to wait and pray. Miriam stayed hidden in the tall reeds and grasses.

After some time passed, Miriam began to worry that the princess would not come to the river's edge.

Suddenly, Miriam heard the chatter of the princess and her servants. Just as the princess was about to step into the water, her gaze settled on the beautiful little basket caught in the reeds.

"Bring me that little boat-shaped basket," she said to her handmaid. The handmaid waded into the reeds and returned with the basket. As she set it on the ground at the princess' feet, soft sounds were heard from inside.

"It's a baby!" exclaimed the princess. "It's an Israelite baby! How can we take care of this little child?" the princess asked her handmaid. "The poor little child must be very hungry."

Miriam thought the princess must have a good and kind heart. So she quietly made her way out of the reeds. Then she bravely asked the princess, "Shall I go and find an Israelite to nurse and take care of this baby for you?"

The princess smiled at Miriam. "Child, if you can bring such a woman to me, I will pay her to care for this baby until he is weaned."

Miriam ran home to tell her mother the good news. Then Miriam and her mother returned to the riverbank as fast as they could.

Jochebed saw the princess with her baby. She could tell that the princess did indeed have a kind heart.

"I will pay you to care for this baby until he is weaned," said the princess. "Then I will raise him as my own. He will be a prince of Egypt."

Jochebed was so happy!

"His name shall be Moses," the princess said. "It means that he was drawn out of the water."

Then the princess gave Jochebed a ring to show to any Egyptian who tried to take the baby. Jochebed and Miriam were filled with hope and happiness. Miriam hugged Moses tightly and thanked God protecting her baby brother.

Moses and Pharaoh

Retold by Brian Conway   Illustrated by Kathy Mitchell

One day, an old man named Shaul said to his grandson Simeon, "It is time you learned the story of our people. I want to tell you about a tragic time for the Israelites, the time we spent in Egypt, and a great man named Moses who saved us from slavery."

Simeon sat at his grandfather's feet and listened to the story.

"I was only a boy then, just about your age," Shaul started. "All of the Israelites were slaves to the terrible Pharaoh, ruler of Egypt. Everyone, even the children, worked all day and into the night, making bricks to build Pharaoh's city.

"One day I saw Moses walking proudly to Pharaoh's palace," said Shaul. "I was such a curious boy then. I dropped my work and crept away. I wanted to hear what Moses had to say.

"Moses asked Pharaoh to let the Israelites go free. He warned Pharaoh that if he did not let them go, God would send a plague. But Pharaoh did nothing. He got up and walked into the palace. Days later I woke up to hear a strange rumbling throughout the city. When I listened more closely, it sounded just like croaking. I looked outside and saw the land was covered with frogs! They were on the roads, on the rooftops, in the wells, and all over Pharaoh's palace!"

"Where did they come from?" Simeon asked his grandfather.

"Moses had warned Pharaoh that many terrible plagues would fall over Egypt if God's people were not set free," Shaul explained. "This was a plague from God. It was not the first sign that God sent to Egypt, and it wouldn't be the last. Pharaoh promised to set the Israelites free if Moses would ask God to take the frogs away. But when the frogs were gone, Pharaoh broke his promise.

"God sent swarms of flies upon Egypt, he made the Egyptians' cattle sick, he pounded the land with hailstorms, and he took away the sunshine. Each time these tragedies fell on Egypt, Moses went to Pharaoh and demanded that he set God's people free. At last God's powers became too much for Pharaoh and his people," Shaul told his grandson. "He agreed to let us leave Egypt. Moses came to bring my family the good news.

"Moses told us to leave as quickly as we could. We did not have time to pack our belongings. We left Egypt with nothing and journeyed into the desert," Shaul said. "It was hot and dry, but at least we were free from Pharaoh and his soldiers. Then one day we saw an army of Egyptians coming after us. Pharaoh had changed his mind again. Pharaoh wanted to bring us back to Egypt. But Moses was our leader, and God was our savior.

"I saw a miracle that day," Shaul added. "With Pharaoh and his men chasing us, we came upon a sea. We had nowhere to turn. Then Moses raised his hand over the sea, and the waters parted.

"Once we had crossed, Moses turned back toward the sea and raised his hand again. The water flowed over Pharaoh and his soldiers.

"We were safe," said Shaul, "and we continued our difficult journey through the desert."

"What happened? How did you survive?" asked Simeon.

"It is not a happy story," said Shaul. "We walked through the hot desert with very little to eat for many years. We suffered greatly, but still we sang to God and prayed, and he provided food for us.

"Then one day Moses told everyone to wait for him, and he climbed up to a mountaintop. Finally Moses returned with two tablets containing the laws that God had spoken to him. They were Ten Commandments from God."

"I know them all, Grandfather," said Simeon proudly. "You taught them to me."

"We followed the laws that God had commanded," Shaul continued. "And we followed Moses as he led us through the desert. God took care of us. He brought us to this place, which we now call Israel. It is our promised land, our country, and our home.

"God watched over his children in the desert," said Shaul. "He watches over us wherever we are. Once we had a great hero, Moses, to remind us of that. Now we have each other. We have the Ten Commandments to guide us, and we have a very important story to tell our children and our grandchildren."

Ruth and Naomi

Retold by Leslie Lindecker   Illustrated by Holly Jones

A man named Elimelech and his wife Naomi traveled from their home in Bethlehem to the country of Moab. They took their two sons, Mahlon and Chilion, with them. They liked Moab and decided to live there. When Mahlon and Chilion grew up, they both married young women from Moab. Their names were Orpah and Ruth. Naomi welcomed the two young women into her home, loving them as her own daughters.

After many years Elimelech became ill and eventually passed away. A few years later Mahlon and Chilion also got sick and died. This left Naomi, Orpah, and Ruth alone and sad. Naomi comforted her daughters-in-law, and they comforted her. Without her husband by her side, Naomi became homesick for the town where she grew up. She decided to return to her home in Bethlehem.

"I love both of you," Naomi told Orpah and Ruth. "But I miss my family in Bethlehem. I would like to return there to live."

Once her belongings were packed, Naomi spoke to Orpah and Ruth. "The two of you should return to your parents," she said. "You can marry again and have children. I am old and will not get married again."

Orpah cried tears of sadness at the thought of leaving Naomi. Naomi had been like a mother to her since she had left home. Orpah kissed Naomi on the cheek. "You have been kind to me," she said. Then Orpah returned to her family's home.

"Do not ask me to leave you," Ruth said to Naomi. "Where you go, I will go. Where you sleep, I will sleep. Your family is my family, and your God is my God."

Naomi saw that Ruth wanted to stay with her. Naomi and Ruth prayed that God would provide for them. Then they began to walk to Bethlehem.

Ruth and Naomi walked for many days to reach Bethlehem. They arrived at the city as the grain harvest began.

Ruth set their bundles down. She turned to Naomi and said, "I will go into the fields. I can gather the grain the men drop. Then we will have grain to pound into flour. I can bake bread for us to eat."

Naomi agreed. "Go, my daughter," she said fondly.

Naomi rested as Ruth went into the fields. The fields were owned by a man named Boaz. Ruth worked behind the reapers, gathering the grain they dropped as they worked. Ruth worked all day.

Late in the afternoon, Boaz came to the field. He greeted his men. "May the Lord be with you," he called to them.

His workers said to him, "May the Lord bless you."

Boaz noticed the young woman following his workers. He called over one of his men. "Who is that woman in the field?" he asked.

"She is from Moab. Her name is Ruth," the worker replied. "She has traveled here with Naomi and asked if she could gather the grain we drop so they would have something to eat."

Boaz watched Ruth. He listened to what his workers told him about Ruth and how she was taking care of Naomi.

Boaz came and spoke to Ruth. "I have heard good things about you. You take care of your mother-in-law. Please continue to work in my fields. When I bring food for my workers, I want you to eat with them," Boaz told her.

"May God bless you and your family," Ruth said.

Boaz said, "Your kindness to Naomi gives me great comfort. I have been told how you lost your husband. Yet you left your mother and father and the country where you were born to take care of Naomi."

When Boaz brought food for his workers, he brought enough for Ruth. Ruth ate with them. She always saved part of her food and took it to Naomi.

Naomi was pleased with the food and the grain. "Who was this man who gave you food and grain?" Naomi asked. Ruth told Naomi about meeting Boaz and what he had said to her.

"Boaz is the brother of my husband," Naomi said. "He is a good man."

Boaz continued to watch Ruth as she worked in his fields each day. He had his reapers drop extra grain as they worked. He wanted Ruth to have plenty of grain to take to Naomi.

Ruth worked in the fields until the end of the harvest time. When the reapers worked, Ruth worked. When the reapers rested, Ruth rested or talked with Boaz. When the reapers ate, Ruth ate, but always saved some of her food for Naomi. Boaz became very fond of Ruth.

Boaz held a celebration when the harvest was over. Naomi said to Ruth, "Put on your best clothes and go to the harvest celebration. Boaz will be there. He is very fond of you. Perhaps he will offer us some security since we are related to him."

Ruth put on her best clothes and went to the celebration. She let Boaz know that she was as fond of him as he was of her.

Boaz was a man of very strong faith. He was also very wise. He knew Naomi and Ruth needed someone to take care of them. He had a younger brother who would be closer to Ruth's age. The next day, Boaz went to his younger brother and addressed him in front of the city elders.

"Naomi has come back to Bethlehem to sell the piece of land which belonged to our brother, Elimelech. I thought you might be interested in buying the piece of land," Boaz said. "If you buy the land, you may also marry Ruth who came back from Moab with Naomi. This way the land will pass on to Elimelech's heirs. If you do not want to buy this piece of land, I will buy it."

His brother was more concerned with losing his own inheritance. "I am not interested in that piece of land. Buy it yourself," he said.

Boaz was very happy his brother said this. He said to the city elders, "I will buy the land from the widow of my brother, Elimelech. I will marry Ruth. She has been working in my fields and taking care of Naomi. She is an honorable woman."

The city elders said, "We are your witnesses. May the Lord bless your house."

Boaz came to Ruth and said, "I would like for you to become my wife. I will buy the land which belonged to my brother, Elimelech. Your mother-in-law, Naomi, may live with us. I will take care of you both."

Ruth was very happy to marry Boaz. She had grown very fond of him. Naomi agreed to come and live with them.

Many friends came to the wedding. Naomi's friends from long ago also came. They were all very happy for Ruth and Boaz.

"How lucky you are, Naomi!" they cried. "You have your daughter-in-law, Ruth, who loves you better than seven sons. God has sent Boaz to take care of you in your old age."

It was not long before Ruth had a baby boy. They named him Obed. Naomi loved her grandson. Obed was the delight of all the family. They all thanked God for their blessings of home and family.

41

Samuel

Retold by Lisa Harkrader   *Illustrated by Jon Goodell*

In the hill country there lived a man named Elkanah. In those days, men could marry more than one woman. Elkanah had married Peninnah and Hannah. Peninnah had given Elkanah many children. But after many years of marriage, Hannah had not been able to give Elkanah even one child. Still, Elkanah loved Hannah very much. He tried to make her happy.

One day, Elkanah saw Hannah playing with Penninah's children. Hannah smiled because the children were having so much fun, but her smile was sad. Elkanah knew Hannah wished she had her own children to play with. He called Hannah over to him.

"It just breaks my heart to see you so sad," he said. "I hope this will cheer you up."

Elkanah gave Hannah a beautiful scarf stitched with threads of gold.

"It's lovely," said Hannah. She tied the scarf around her head. "Thank you."

Peninnah saw the gift Elkanah had given Hannah. She waited until Elkanah had left, then went over to see Hannah's new scarf.

"You know why Elkanah gave it to you," Peninnah said.

Hannah frowned. "He said he wanted to cheer me up."

"After all these years, you haven't been able to give Elkanah any children. Don't you think that upsets him?" asked Peninnah.

"Well, yes," said Hannah. "I'm sure it does."

"Of course it does," said Peninnah. "He doesn't give you these gifts because he loves you. He can't possibly love a woman who has disappointed him so. He's only nice to you because he feels sorry for you."

Over the years, Peninnah had more children. Hannah did not understand why God had not given her a child, too.

Finally, in anguish, Hannah traveled to Shiloh to pray in God's temple. She fell on her knees and clasped her hands tightly together.

"Please, God," she whispered. "I want a baby with all my heart. If you could see fit to give me a son, I promise that he will spend his life serving you."

Hannah prayed for such a long time that the priest of the temple, Eli, noticed her. He came over to where she was kneeling and asked her if she was ill.

Hannah shook her head. "I'm not ill," she said, "but something is very wrong. I have tried for so long to have a baby, but so far God has not blessed me with a child. I'm praying for a baby now. I want to give my husband a son."

"I understand," said Eli. "How very sad you must be." He blessed her, then he said, "Go in peace, and may the God of Israel give you what you have asked for."

Then Hannah traveled back to her home in the hills and waited. Hannah soon discovered she was going to have a baby!

"I want to name him Samuel," said Hannah when the baby was born. "It means asked of the Lord. Our son was born because I asked God."

"Then Samuel will be his name," said Elkanah.

Samuel grew to be a strong and healthy boy. His mother loved him and took good care of him. But she did not forget what she had told God. She did not forget her promise that her son would serve God all of his life.

So when Samuel was old enough, Hannah and Elkanah took him to the temple in Shiloh, the same temple where Hannah had prayed for a child. There they found the temple priest, Eli.

"God has given me what I wanted," Hannah told Eli. "And now I will give God what I promised."

She kissed Samuel and held him tight. "You must live in the temple with Eli now," she said. "He will take care of you and teach you to serve God."

Hannah and Elkanah left Samuel with Eli and traveled back to their home in the hills. Once a year they returned to Shiloh to visit Samuel and worship God in the temple. Hannah always brought Samuel a fine new coat she had made.

God blessed Hannah again. In the next few years, Hannah and Elkanah had five more children.

Samuel helped Eli and learned as much as he could about serving God and being a priest. Samuel grew up to be an honest and hardworking man.

Eli had two sons who lived in the temple, too. These sons were not honest like Samuel. They were greedy and sneaky.

One night, after Samuel had gone to bed, he heard someone call his name. He thought it must be Eli, so he knelt down beside Eli's bed.

"I'm here," said Samuel. "Why did you call me?"

Eli woke up and rubbed his eyes. "I didn't call you, Samuel. Go back to bed."

Samuel went back to his bed, but again he heard someone call his name. So he went to Eli.

"I heard you call," he said. "Do you need me?"

"I didn't call you," said Eli.

Samuel went back to bed, but he heard someone call his name again.

Samuel rose from his bed a third time, and for a third time he asked Eli why he had called.

"I didn't call you," said Eli. "God must be calling you. Go back to your bed and say, 'Speak, Lord. I am your servant, and I am listening.'"

Samuel went back to bed. He was frightened because he did not know what God would want to tell him. But he trusted God, and he did as Eli told him.

"Speak, Lord," said Samuel. "I am your servant, and I am listening."

God spoke to him. "Eli's sons have brought shame to the temple," God said. "I will not allow them to take Eli's place as temple priests."

The next morning Samuel told Eli what God had said.

Eli shook his head sadly. "It's true," he said. "My sons do not honor God. You, Samuel, will become the temple priest."

Eli was a very old man. When he died, Samuel took his place at the temple. God spoke to Samuel many times, and everything God told him came true.

Samuel had sons of his own by this time. But just like Eli's sons, they had become sneaky and greedy. In those days, the priests ruled Israel by following God. The people of Israel loved Samuel, but they knew someday his sons would take his place as the temple priests. They did not want to be ruled by greedy men who did not honor God.

"Other nations are ruled by a king," they said. "We want a king to rule us, too."

Samuel was horrified. "But Israel isn't like other nations," he said. "God is Israel's king. God speaks to his people through his priests."

"Not all priests honor God like you do, Samuel," the people said. "God will not speak to us through priests who bring shame to the temple. We need a king."

Samuel did not know what to do. He prayed to God.

"Give the people what they want," God said. "Tomorrow I will send a young man from the land of Benjamin. He will become the king of Israel."

The next day, a young man arrived at the temple. He was tall and strong.

"My name is Saul," the young man said. "I am from the tribe of Benjamin. I'm looking for some donkeys that escaped from my father's herd."

Samuel blessed Saul and proclaimed him the first king of Israel. But Samuel did not want the people of Israel to forget to follow God's laws. He called the people of Israel together.

"If you and your king serve the Lord he will not abandon you," Samuel said.

Samuel knew that what he told the people of Israel was true. His mother had trusted and served God all her life. Samuel, too, had trusted and served God all his life. And God had never abandoned them.

David and Goliath

Retold by Virginia Biles   *Illustrated by Douglas Klauba*

When Saul was the king of the Israelites, he did some wicked acts that made God unhappy with him. God said to him, "Saul, because you have followed your own wishes and not listened to me, I will choose another man to be the king of Israel."

Then God told Samuel, who was a prophet, "Go to the home of Jesse in Bethlehem. There you will find the next king of Israel. Anoint his head with oil. Tell him that I have chosen him to lead the people of Israel."

Samuel was afraid that King Saul would be angry with him and kill him if he did what God wanted. But God said, "Pretend you are going to Bethlehem to make a religious offering to me. Invite Jesse and his sons to come to see you." Samuel was still afraid, but he did what God asked.

Jesse's oldest son was tall and good looking. Samuel thought, "This is the one that God wants to be the king."

God said, "I am not looking at his appearance, I am looking at his heart. He is not the one."

48

Samuel then called the second son and the third. They were not the chosen ones either. "Do you have more sons?" asked Samuel.

"I have one more son," Jesse said. "But he is still just a young boy. He is out tending the sheep."

"Call him," said Samuel.

When the boy David appeared, God said, "This is my chosen one."

Samuel poured a little sweet smelling oil on David's head and said to him, "Someday you will be the king of Israel."

King Saul became sick because of his wickedness. His servants thought that some soft music would help their master, so they looked for someone who could play the harp. One of them knew that a boy in Bethlehem named David, son of Jesse, could play the harp. King Saul's servants sent for David.

For several more months, whenever King Saul's head ached and he grew sad, he called for David.

"Play and sing for me," he said. David sang in his clear, sweet voice and played his harp. King Saul covered his eyes with his hand, and the pain left his body. King Saul grew to love the small boy.

After a while, David returned home to care for his father's sheep. He made sure none of the sheep wandered off or got eaten by wild animals.

He would sit by the flock of sheep and play his harp and sing to them. His beautiful music made the sheep very peaceful and calm.

One day, a lion crept down from the hills and sprang on a sheep. The lion grabbed the sheep in his strong jaws and started dragging it to the underbrush.

David heard the sheep bleating. He dropped his harp and grabbed his sling and bag of stones from his belt. He ran toward the lion and the crying sheep, all the while placing a single smooth rock in the fold of his sling.

Quickly and surely, he swung the sling over his head. The sling whistled in the air. Then David let the stone fly through the air. The stone hit the lion right on the forehead. The lion fell to the ground.

The sheep, loosened from the lion's powerful jaws, scampered away. Then David killed the fierce lion.

Another day a bear tried to kill a sheep. David killed the bear in the same way he had killed the lion.

During this same time, King Saul was at war with the Philistines. David's three older brothers were soldiers in King Saul's army. One day David's father, Jesse, sent for David.

"I want you to go to the army camp," David's father said, "and take some grain and bread to your brothers. Find out how they are doing."

So David got up early in the morning, left his flock with another shepherd, and walked the miles to the soldiers' camp. When he arrived, he found the two armies lined up facing each other.

David went to the battle line to find his brothers. While he was talking to them, a fierce giant stepped out of the Philistine line.

The giant called to King Saul's soldiers, "I am a Philistine, and you are soldiers of Saul. Choose a man yourselves and let him fight me. If I win, you shall become our servants. If your man wins, we shall become your servants."

King Saul's men were afraid of the giant man named Goliath. Not only was he almost as large as two men, he was fierce-looking. He wore a bronze helmet on his head, and his chest was covered in bronze armor that looked like large fish scales. He also carried a spear.

David thought to himself, "With the help of God I can defeat the giant."

Then David told Saul's soldiers, "I can kill the giant."

When King Saul heard of David's boast, he called for David to be brought to him.

"You are just a boy with no experience," he said. "Why do you think you can kill the giant?"

"With God's help I killed a lion and a bear. The same God who saved me from the lion and the bear will save me from Goliath," said David.

King Saul believed that the boy might save the army of God. He called for his armor. He helped David put on armor that would protect him from Goliath's spear.

"I cannot wear this armor," David said. "It is too heavy."

Instead of wearing King Saul's armor, David chose stones from a nearby stream. David weighed each one in his hand until he had five perfect stones. He placed the stones in the pouch at his waist. Then, with his sling in his hand, he approached the giant Goliath.

When Goliath saw David walking toward him, he laughed. He could not believe that King Saul would send a boy to fight him.

"Come on, boy," the giant said. "I will feed you to the wild animals!"

David looked at the giant. Then he looked toward the heavens. "You may have a sword, a spear, and a javelin," he called to Goliath, "but I have the Lord on my side. The Lord and I will defeat you!"

With an angry roar, Goliath lifted his spear and ran toward David. David ran to meet him. David reached into his pouch, drew out one of his carefully chosen round stones, and placed it in his sling. Then he swung it over his head. The stone flew through the air.

Before Goliath realized what was happening, the stone struck him in the middle of his forehead. Goliath's spear fell to the ground in front of David. Then Goliath spread his arms and fell face down on the ground with a thud.

King Saul's men cheered and rushed forward to claim the victory. King Saul, watching from the battle line, called out, "Who is that boy's father? Bring the boy to me so I can thank him." He must have wondered if David's father was a warrior, but David was just a shepherd boy whom God loved. Saul made David a leader of his men. After Saul died, David became the king.

The Fiery Furnace

Retold by Kate Hannigan   Illustrated by Winson Trang

Nebuchadnezzar was the king of Babylon. One day, he decided to make a big golden statue and put it out for everyone to see. He called all the officials in all the land to come and admire his big golden statue.

King Nebuchadnezzar said, "The moment you hear music playing you must fall to your knees and worship my golden statue. I warn you, whoever does not fall to his knees and worship the golden statue will be thrown into a blazing furnace!"

When the time was right, King Nebuchadnezzar signaled the musicians to play. The sounds of their flutes, horns, and harps filled the hall where all the officials were gathered. The officials fell to their knees to worship the golden statue.

Just then, the king's messenger ran to the throne. The messenger told the king that not everyone had followed his orders.

"My king," the messenger said, "Shadrach, Meshach, and Abednego did not bow down to the statue."

King Nebuchadnezzar became very angry. He stomped his feet and waved his fists at the messenger. "Go get Shadrach, Meshach, and Abednego and bring them to me!" he yelled.

Shadrach, Meshach, and Abednego were brought before King Nebuchadnezzar. "Is it true that you do not serve my gods or worship the golden image that I have made?" King Nebuchadnezzar asked.

The three men nodded their heads.

"If you do not fall to your knees," King Nebuchadnezzar said, "I will have no choice but to throw you into a blazing fire. What god is there who can deliver you out of my hands?"

Shadrach, Meshach, and Abednego were not afraid. They did not shake before the angry king but stood tall together. They told King Nebuchadnezzar that their God was able to deliver them from the blazing fire. He would also deliver them from the king's hands.

"Even if he does not," they said, "we will not serve your gods. We will not fall to our knees before your golden statue."

King Nebuchadnezzar became very angry with the three men. He ordered his servants to make the fire seven times hotter. Then King Nebuchadnezzar ordered his strongest soldiers to tie up Shadrach, Meshach, and Abednego and throw them into the fiery furnace.

The soldiers bound the feet and arms of the three men and tossed them into the red and orange flames. But since it was seven times hotter than usual, the fire burned the king's soldiers.

As King Nebuchadnezzar watched the furnace, he did not believe what he saw. "Didn't we throw three men into the fire? And weren't they tied up?" he asked.

King Nebuchadnezzar pointed his finger at the blazing hot fire, and his jaw dropped. He could see four men in the middle of the flames. The men were not tied up! They were walking around the furnace.

King Nebuchadnezzar ran to the door of the blazing furnace. Then he ordered Shadrach, Meshach, and Abednego to come out.

Shadrach, Meshach, and Abednego bravely walked out of the flames and were not hurt. Their clothes were not burned, not a single hair on their heads was harmed, and they did not even smell like smoke.

King Nebuchadnezzar raised his hands into the air and said, "Blessed be the God of Shadrach, Meshach, and Abednego!"

Then King Nebuchadnezzar turned to the crowd and said, "God sent an angel to deliver Shadrach, Meshach, and Abednego from the fire."

All the officials turned to each other and began talking wildly.

"We have witnessed a miracle!" some exclaimed.

"There is no other god who could deliver these men safely from the fire," King Nebuchadnezzar said. He quickly declared that anyone who talked badly about God would be punished.

Shadrach, Meshach, and Abednego left the king that day. They all lived happy lives in Babylon.

Daniel in the Lions' Den

Retold by Virginia Biles   *Illustrated by Cathy Johnson*

When Daniel was a young boy, his country, Judah, was conquered by King Nebuchadnezzar. Daniel's people, who were Jews, were taken as prisoners to Babylon. They lived there for many years. Daniel was also a prisoner, but he was taken to the king's palace to live. All the smart young men went to live at the king's palace. He planned to teach them all about their new country and to make them great leaders. Daniel and his friends were happy in their new home, but Daniel continued to worship God.

God was pleased with Daniel as he grew into a young man. God rewarded him by giving him a special gift. Daniel could interpret dreams.

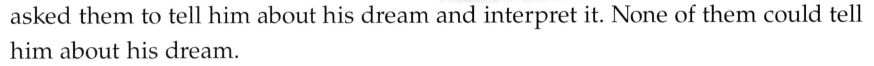

One night the king had a dream, but when he woke up he could not remember it. He called his wise men together and asked them to tell him about his dream and interpret it. None of them could tell him about his dream.

When Daniel heard this he said, "I will go to the king. God has given me a gift. I can interpret dreams and visions."

Daniel told the king what he had dreamed and what it meant. The king was so pleased that he placed Daniel in a high position and gave him many gifts.

Later the king sent for Daniel again. He told Daniel about another dream.

Daniel said, "It means that you will live with the wild animals and eat grass like a cow. You will do this for seven years until you follow God."

King Nebuchadnezzar laughed. "I will never live with the wild animals," he said. "I am a great king. I built the beautiful palace of Babylon!"

God was not happy with this king who was so full of pride. No sooner were the words out of his mouth than he became like an animal. He tore his clothes. He ran away to the woods and lived with the wild animals. His hair grew long, and his nails were like the claws of a bird.

At the end of seven long years, King Nebuchadnezzar praised God. Then God returned his mind to him. He spent the rest of his days praising God.

When King Nebuchadnezzar died, his son Belshazzar became the king. One night during a banquet, the king and his guests saw ghostly fingers writing on the wall of the dining room. The king's face grew very pale, and his knees grew weak. There was no body, hand, or arm—the king only saw pale ghostly fingers.

King Belshazzar called for his astrologers. "What does this mean?" he asked them. When they could not tell him, he grew even paler and more frightened. Then someone remembered Daniel.

The king sent for Daniel. "What does this mean?" King Belshazzar asked. "If you can tell me I will make you the third highest ruler in the kingdom and give you riches."

"It means that your kingdom will be taken by your enemies," Daniel said. That very night, King Belshazzar was killed in battle and his kingdom was taken by King Darius.

King Darius had heard of wise Daniel, and he made him one of his top three rulers. He even planned to make him his top advisor.

The other wise men were jealous of Daniel, and they wanted to get rid of him. They went to King Darius. "Your wise men have all agreed that you should make a law that declares that anyone who prays to any god or man, except you, during the next thirty days will be thrown into the lions' den. No one can change this law."

King Darius thought this was a good idea, and he made it a law. When Daniel heard about the new law he prayed to God, just as he had done before the law.

The wise men sent one of their own men to spy on Daniel. The spy listened at Daniel's door and heard him praying to God.

The spy carried this news back to the other wise men. They now had the proof they needed to harm Daniel, which they presented to King Darius.

"You made a law that states that during the next thirty days anyone who prays to a god will be thrown into the lions' den," the wise men said. "Daniel still prays three times a day. We have seen and heard him."

King Darius did not want to kill Daniel, but he had made the law. "I will change the law," he said. "I am the king."

His wise men reminded him that the law could not be changed. King Darius was very sad. He knew that he had been tricked by his wise men. "Bring Daniel to me," the king ordered.

The soldiers marched up the marble stairs to Daniel's room. Daniel could hear their armor clanging as they came near, and he knew that they were coming for him. He fell to his knees and prayed, "God, please protect me."

When King Darius saw Daniel with his wrists tied, he was sorry that he had made the law. He knew he could not change the law and that he would have to throw Daniel into the lions' den.

King Darius put his hand on Daniel's shoulder and said, "May your God rescue you from the lions."

The soldiers led Daniel from the palace and through the streets. King Darius followed behind, riding on a chair carried by his servants. The wise men stood on the balcony of the palace and watched Daniel being led away. They smiled to each other because their plan had worked. They would not have to worry about Daniel any longer.

Up into the hills they marched. There were rocks and caves in the hills. In one cave was a deep pit. It held hungry lions. The soldiers stopped at this cave. They could hear the roar of the lions deep within the pit, and they were frightened.

The soldiers shoved Daniel into the cave. He fell into the pit with the lions. King Darius could hear the roaring lions, and he could smell the terrible odor coming from the pit. Then the soldiers rolled a large rock in front of the mouth of the cave.

King Darius sealed the entrance to the cave. No one could rescue Daniel. King Darius slowly climbed onto his chair and went back to the palace.

All night long, King Darius walked back and forth. He could not sleep. All he could think about was Daniel being eaten by the hungry lions.

At dawn, King Darius called two of his soldiers and hurried on foot to the lions' den. He put his face close to the rock and called loudly, "Daniel! Daniel! Has your God rescued you from the lions? Are you still alive?"

He listened carefully, afraid that he would not hear anything but the lions' roar.

Then a voice said, "Yes, I am alive. God sent his angel, and he shut the lions' mouths. The lions have not hurt me because I am innocent in God's sight. I have never wronged you either."

The king ordered his to soldiers roll the rock away from the mouth of the cave, and Daniel was lifted from the den.

Daniel stood before King Darius. Not a scratch was on him. King Darius was overjoyed to see that Daniel was safe.

King Darius took Daniel back to the palace, and he became the king's most trusted advisor. Over the rest of his life, he interpreted many dreams and visions for the king.

King Darius punished the men who had accused Daniel by closing them in the lions' den, but God did not send an angel to help them.

Jonah and the Whale

Retold by Michelle Conway   *Illustrated by Tom Newsom*

One day, God came to Jonah and asked him to be his messenger. The people in Nineveh were making God very unhappy. All the people had forgotten about God and what he wanted them to do. God asked Jonah to bring his message to these people. God said, "Go to Nineveh. Tell the people that they have made me very angry. Tell them to change their ways or I will destroy their city."

Jonah was from Israel, and the people of Nineveh were his enemies. Jonah did not want to go there. So Jonah went in the opposite direction.

"I will hide from God," Jonah said.

Soon, Jonah arrived in Joppa. He walked through the crowds of people. But he still thought God might find him. So then he looked for a ship that would take him to a faraway land called Tarshish.

Jonah looked out into the sea. He noticed some men loading a ship. Jonah ran across the sand to the men. "Are you going to Tarshish?" he asked the men. The men nodded. Jonah paid the men his fare and climbed aboard the ship.

"Surely, God will not find me in Tarshish," Jonah said. Then Jonah climbed down into the hull of the ship. He wanted to find a place to rest.

A short time later, the captain of the ship gave orders to his men. They were leaving the harbor and setting out to sea. The waters were calm and the sky was blue. It was a perfect day for sailing.

Once they were out to sea, dark clouds rolled in from the east and the west. The boat began to sway back and forth as the waves grew. A great storm swept over the sea. Rain poured from the dark sky. A strong wind rocked the boat harder.

One man began throwing the cargo into the sea. The other men followed. They were hoping a lighter ship would help them make it through the great storm.

The captain looked around the ship. He did not see Jonah. He climbed down into the hull of the ship to find him.

The captain approached Jonah. "Why are you sleeping?" he asked. "You must call on your God to save us from this storm."

The sailors above shouted to one another. "Someone has brought this storm upon us," they said. They decided to cast lots to see who was responsible for the storm.

The captain brought Jonah to the deck of the ship. One sailor broke a broom handle into many splinters. He held them in his hand as each man chose one. Jonah was the last to choose. When he looked down at his hand, Jonah knew he had chosen the largest stick.

The great storm was Jonah's fault. God was punishing him for running away.

Jonah explained why he had run away from God. The sailors became even more frightened. One man stepped forward. "What should we do to calm the sea?" he asked. The waves were getting bigger as he spoke.

Jonah realized he could not hide from God any longer. So he told them to throw him into the sea. "Then the sea will become quiet for you," he said.

The men did not want to throw Jonah into the sea. They tried to row back to the shore. But the winds were too strong, and the waves were too large.

Finally the sailors picked up Jonah and threw him into the water.

At once, the sea stopped raging. The winds died down, and the sky became bright again.

The sailors thought of Jonah swimming in the sea. They worried about him, but they thanked God for their safety.

Jonah was floating in the sea when a giant whale swam up behind him. In one mighty gulp, the whale swallowed Jonah. Jonah lived in the belly of the whale for three days and three nights.

During this time, Jonah prayed to God. "I called you when I was in trouble," he said. "And you answered me. When you call me again, I will answer you." Then Jonah thanked God for letting him live.

God heard Jonah's prayers. He knew that Jonah was sorry for disobeying him and running away.

God gave the great whale a command. The fish swam close to shore, opened its mouth, and tossed Jonah onto dry land.

"Get up and go to Nineveh," God said. "Bring my message to the people." This time Jonah obeyed God.

When Jonah reached the busy city, he began crying out to the people. "In forty days, God will destroy the city of Nineveh," he said. "You must change all your wicked ways."

Soon the people of Nineveh believed Jonah's words. And they believed in God. They were afraid for their city. The people stopped eating to show their devotion to God. They wore rags to show God they were sorry.

Finally Jonah's words reached the king of Nineveh. He rose from his throne, took off his royal robes, and put on rags like the people of Nineveh.

The king ordered the people to ask God for forgiveness. The people did as they were told. God heard their prayers. God forgave the people and saved their city.

"Why did you make me travel all this way?" Jonah asked God. "I knew that you would never destroy the city."

"Do you have a reason to be angry?" asked God. Jonah did not answer.

Jonah left the city. He walked for a long time, then decided to rest. God made a thick vine grow above Jonah's head. It shaded all of him from the burning sun.

The next morning, God sent a worm to attack the plant. Soon the vine withered and died. Jonah awoke and found the vine lying on the ground. Then he saw the green worm crawling on one of the dead branches.

Later in the day, God sent the sun to beat down on Jonah's head. Jonah became so weak that he asked God to let him die.

"Do you have good reason to be angry about the plant?" God asked Jonah.

"Yes," said Jonah. "I am angry enough to die."

"You loved that plant even though you did not grow it," God said. "You must understand, it was only alive for one day. I have loved the people of Nineveh for years. I cannot destroy something so great.

"How can you be sad over the death of a vine," God asked, "but not sad over the death of everyone in Nineveh?"

Jonah understood that God forgives anyone who turns to him. Jonah was very thankful for God's forgiveness.

Jesus' Birth

Retold by Rebecca Grazulis   *Illustrated by Jane Maday*

Many years ago, God sent the angel Gabriel to speak to Mary. "Hail, Mary!" exclaimed Gabriel. "The Lord is with you."

"Why have you come to see me?" asked Mary.

"Do not be afraid," Gabriel told Mary kindly. "You have found great favor with God. You will soon have a son, and you shall name the child Jesus."

"A son?" asked a frightened Mary.

"Yes," replied Gabriel. "He will be great and will be called the Son of the Most High. His kingdom will have no end."

"How can this be?" asked Mary. "I am not yet married."

"The Holy Spirit will come upon you," Gabriel said. "And your son will be called the Son of God."

Mary did not know what to say. Could this all be true?

But Gabriel had even more good news to share.

"Your cousin Elizabeth is also with child in her old age," said Gabriel. "For nothing is impossible with God."

After Gabriel left, Mary went into her home to gather some things before going to visit Elizabeth. She wanted to share her news with her cousin. And she wanted to help Elizabeth get ready to have her baby.

The time came for Elizabeth to give birth. She had a son. Her neighbors and family rejoiced with her. They wanted to name the child Zacharias, after his father. But Elizabeth had another idea.

"He shall be called John," announced Elizabeth.

During this time, an angel appeared to Joseph in a dream. Joseph and Mary were supposed to be wed. But when he heard that Mary was with child, he became very scared.

"Joseph," said the angel, "do not be afraid to take Mary as your wife. The baby she carries is from the Holy Spirit. She will have a son and you will call him Jesus. He will save people from their sins."

Joseph arose from his sleep. He remembered what the angel had told him and bravely took Mary as his wife.

In those days, it came about that Caesar Augustus ordered that a census be taken. Soon all people were registering for the census in their own cities. Joseph and Mary went to Bethlehem to register.

While Joseph and Mary were in Bethlehem, it came time for Mary to give birth. They went from inn to inn looking for a place to stay.

There did not seem to be a place for Joseph and Mary to go. They were tired, and the sun was beginning to set. Mary was sitting on a donkey, and Joseph was leading the animal down a dusty road. Then Joseph saw one last inn. He decided to speak to the innkeeper, hoping he would have a room.

"Please sir," said Joseph, "we will take any room. My wife, Mary, needs a place to sleep."

"There is no more room at the inn tonight," said the innkeeper, "but you could stay in the stable. The animals are in there, but it is warm and the hay is soft."

Joseph and Mary thanked the man and made their way to the stable. Before long, Mary had given birth to her firstborn son. Mary wrapped the baby lovingly in swaddling clothes and laid him down in the manger.

There were many animals in the stable. When they heard the baby's cries, they made noises to welcome Jesus into the world.

Nearby there were some shepherds out in the fields keeping watch over their flocks. An angel soon appeared to them. The shepherds were very frightened.

Then the angel said, "Do not be afraid. I bring you good news of a great joy. Today in Bethlehem a child has been born. He is the Savior for all people. The child is Christ the Lord. You will find the baby wrapped in swaddling clothes and lying in a manger," said the angel.

At that moment, many angels appeared before the shepherds. They were all praising God and celebrating the birth of Jesus.

"Glory to God in the highest," they sang, "and peace to his people on earth."

The shepherds quickly made their way to Bethlehem. Soon they found Mary and Joseph in the stable.

"We are humble shepherds," they began. "An angel came to us and told us of your child's birth. The angel told us that your baby is the Savior."

Mary looked lovingly at her little child. She knew in her heart that what the shepherds said was true.

"Thank you for coming to welcome our child into the world," she replied.

A while later, the shepherds went back to their fields. As they walked, they praised God for everything they had seen. They knew the baby was the Savior.

Now, at about the same time, three wise men from the east saw the bright star that hung over the stable. They had heard that this was a sign that Christ had been born. So they followed the star until they came to Bethlehem.

"This must be where the Christ Child is!" they exclaimed.

When they saw the Christ Child they fell to their knees. They brought the child gold, frankincense, and myrrh.

After the wise men left, an angel came to Joseph in a dream. "Arise and take Mary and the child to Egypt," said the angel. "They will be safe there."

Joseph did as he was told. Mary and Joseph journeyed through the night. They stayed in Egypt until another angel appeared to Joseph in a dream.

"Arise," said the angel. "Take the child and his mother and go into the land of Israel. It is safe now."

Joseph and Mary settled in a place called Nazareth. The baby came to be known as Jesus of Nazareth.

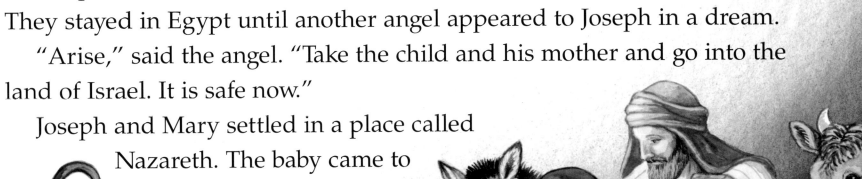

Jesus' Baptism

Retold by Michelle Conway *Illustrated by Renée Daily*

John the Baptist wandered through the forest each day. He ate berries and locusts. At night, he slept under a canopy of branches. John was happy living in the wilderness.

John was living in the wilderness to be closer to God. He wanted to follow God and obey his rules.

Even though John lived in the wilderness, he still spoke to many people in Judea about God.

"The kingdom of God is at hand," John told the people. "The Messiah will soon appear."

John brought God's message to the people. He wanted them to be sorry for all of their sins. God wanted John to baptize the people. John listened carefully and obeyed God.

John began preaching in the country surrounding the Jordan River. "You must confess your sins," he told the people. "Come to the river to be baptized." Soon the people listened and followed John to the river.

John wore a cloak made from camel's hair. He even ate wild honey. He was very different, but people listened to him. People from all over were coming to the Jordan River to be baptized by John.

When the first group of people arrived at the river, John asked them, "Why have you come?" He wanted to make sure the people were coming to confess their sins.

"We have come to confess all of our sins" the people said.

John told the people by the river how to live better lives. He told them to follow all of God's laws.

One man came forward to be baptized. "I am ready to confess," he said.

John led the man into the river. He gathered some water in his hand and poured it over the man's head. At the same time, John said, "I baptize you in the name of God the Father."

The people in the crowd thought John was so wise. They began to wonder if he was the Messiah. "Could he be the one we've been waiting for?" they asked.

But John said, "I baptize you with water, but someone will come who is much more powerful than me. He will baptize you with the Holy Spirit."

John continued to baptize the people until he heard some of them whispering. The crowd parted as a man walked toward the river.

The mysterious man waded into the river up to his knees. He stopped in front of John the Baptist. "I have come to be baptized by you," he said.

John fell to his knees and bowed his head. The stranger put his hand on John's shoulder.

"It must be Jesus," the people said.

"Will you please baptize me, John?" Jesus asked.

"I am not worthy," John said.

"God has chosen you," said Jesus.

"You should be the one baptizing me," John said. Then he put his hand on Jesus' shoulder. "But I will be honored to baptize you," John said.

John gathered water in his hand and poured it over Jesus' head. "In the name of God the Father, I baptize you," he said. Jesus bowed to pray.

Just then, the clouds opened up. The sun shone down on Jesus. A white dove flew from the sky. It hovered above Jesus' head.

Jesus smiled and said to all the people, "This is the Holy Spirit. God has sent this beautiful bird because he is pleased. He loves me just as he loves all of you."

After Jesus was baptized, more people came forward. They wanted John to baptize them, too.

It was time for Jesus to begin teaching people about God. He traveled around the land telling people to confess their sins.

Fishers of Men

Retold by Michelle Conway   *Illustrated by Thea Kliros*

Jesus was a teacher. He traveled throughout the land teaching people about God. One day, Jesus was standing on the shore of Lake Gennesaret. People gathered around him to hear his message. While he was speaking, Jesus looked out onto the water. He saw two boats resting near the shore.

The fishermen were standing next to their boats. Their heads hung low as they washed out their empty nets. "Another day without a catch," said one man.

Jesus heard the men talking and began walking toward their boats. The crowd followed Jesus and waited for him to speak. He climbed into one of the boats and asked, "Whose boat is this?"

"That is my boat," said a man named Simon.

Jesus asked Simon to push the boat away from shore. Jesus climbed into the boat with Simon and the other fishermen. Then they pushed the boat out into the water. Soon Jesus began teaching the crowd from the boat.

When he was finished speaking, Jesus said to Simon, "Let your nets down for a great catch."

Simon did not believe Jesus. "Sir, we have worked hard all night," he said. "We have caught nothing, but we will let down our nets for you."

Simon and the fishermen let down their nets. Suddenly, the nets were bulging with fish. The nets were so full, they began to break! The other fishermen helped Simon gather the fish in their boats. Soon the boats were so full, they almost sank.

Simon fell down at Jesus' feet and said, "Please forgive me for not believing."

"Do not fear," said Jesus. "From now on you will be catching men." With that, the fishermen left their boats and followed Jesus. They watched him teach in many different cities.

One day, Jesus went into the mountains to pray. When morning came, he called the fishermen to his side. "I have chosen you to become my disciples," Jesus said.

The men all looked very surprised. "You must spread my message to all the people. And remember, always treat people the way you would like to be treated," Jesus reminded them. Then Jesus and the disciples left to spread God's message to anyone who would listen.

Feeding the Multitude

Retold by Leslie Lindecker   Illustrated by Victoria and Julius Lisi

Jesus and his disciples wanted to go to a quiet place to pray and talk. They found a boat and decided to sail away from town. The people of the town by the lake recognized Jesus. They had heard of his miracles and of the stories he told.

The people wanted to be with Jesus. They wanted to hear what he had to say. They wanted to see Jesus heal the sick and injured people. They ran along the shore of the lake as the boat sailed across the water.

When Jesus and his disciples reached the other side of the lake, thousands of people were waiting for them. The people waiting to hear Jesus speak stood as far as the tops of the hills surrounding the lake. Jesus felt their love for him as soon as his boat touched the shore. He felt love for all of these people, too.

Jesus stepped out of the boat and began to talk to the people. Jesus began to tell them wonderful stories about God.

Jesus talked to the people all day long. People who had a special need were helped. People who were hurting were healed.

Late in the afternoon the disciples came to Jesus and said, "You must send all of these people home. There is no food here for them to eat."

Jesus said to the disciples, "Do not send these people away. They have come to be with us. You must give them something to eat!"

The disciples were worried. "Teacher," they said, "shall we go back to the town in the boat and buy food for all these people? We only have a little bit of money. There are over five thousand people here."

"What food do you have?" Jesus asked. The disciples did not have any food with them. They began to look for any food they could find among all the people listening to Jesus.

"There is a young boy who has five loaves of bread," they said. "And he has two fish he caught in the lake. The rest of the people who came here to listen to you did not bring any food with them. This bit of food is not enough to feed all these people."

Jesus said, "Bring the young boy to me. We will ask him to share his meal."

The disciples brought the young boy to Jesus. Jesus asked him, "Would you share your five loaves of bread and two fish with all the people here?"

The young boy answered Jesus. "Yes, I am happy to share with you. But this is hardly enough to feed my family. How can my small loaves and fish feed all the people here?"

The young boy handed Jesus the bread and the fish. Jesus stepped away from the disciples. He held the loaves and the two fish in his hands. Jesus' disciples and the young boy bowed their heads. The crowd of people became silent as Jesus prayed.

"Thank you, God, for this food you have given us," Jesus prayed. "Bless these five loaves of bread and two fish as you have blessed each of us. Amen."

Then Jesus told the disciples to divide the crowd into small groups. Jesus broke the five loaves of bread into pieces. "Give everyone as much bread as they can eat," Jesus said.

Then Jesus divided the fish. "Take these pieces of fish and share them with all the people. Give everyone as much fish as they can eat," Jesus said.

The disciples walked among all the groups of people sitting on the ground. They shared the bread and the fish. Everyone had as much fish and bread as they could possibly eat.

When everyone was full, Jesus said to the disciples, "Take the baskets from our boat and gather all the leftover bread and fish."

Once again the disciples walked among the groups of people sitting on the ground. They gathered the leftover bread and fish.

When they were done, not a crumb was left on the ground. The disciples brought twelve baskets of leftover food to Jesus.

The crowd knew they had witnessed true miracles that day. Jesus had told them stories about God's love. He had healed the sick and injured people who came to him. Jesus took five loaves of bread and two fish and fed over five thousand people until they were full.

The people began to rejoice. Now they truly believed that Jesus was the Son of God. They had witnessed his miracles with their own eyes. Many of these people went out into other villages and towns to share what they had seen. Each person felt blessed by God.

Jesus Walks on Water

Retold by Lynne Suesse   Illustrated by Mark Stephens

Jesus performed many miracles. He always did what was right. He tried to teach other people to do what was right, too. He put the feelings of other people before his own feelings. He helped many people.

One day, Jesus had performed a miracle. He had fed thousands of people with only two fish and five loaves of bread. His friends, the disciples, were amazed at what Jesus did. They thought that Jesus should have sent the people home without any dinner.

The next day, Jesus wanted to be alone to pray. He told his disciples that they should set off for a new land. He told them to take a boat and sail across the water. Jesus said that he would follow them in a short while.

Then Jesus began to climb a mountain. It was a long journey. Jesus stopped a few times to look at the ground beneath him. He watched the colors change on the trees as the sun began to set.

Upon reaching the top of the mountain, Jesus sat down to pray. He prayed for hours.

At the bottom of the mountain, the disciples were worried about Jesus. They did not want to leave him on the mountain all by himself. But they listened to what he said and left him alone. It was important for Jesus to be by himself to pray.

"Jesus wants to be alone," said Luke. "We should do what he wants."

The disciples prepared the boat to set sail. As the disciples drifted on the water, they spoke of the miracles they had witnessed.

Up on the mountain, Jesus prayed all night. He watched the sky grow very dark and then begin to become light again. It was very early in the morning when Jesus had finished praying. He knew that he must meet the disciples, as he said that he would. Jesus began to walk down from the mountain.

Once at the bottom of the mountain, Jesus looked across the water to find his disciples. The sky looked stormy, and the water was rough. It was hard to see. After a moment, he saw the disciples in their boat. He could see that the boat was in trouble. It was being tossed by the waves and wind. Jesus knew that he had to help them.

The water was very choppy, and sharp rocks were close to the disciples' boat. If the boat hit the rocks, the disciples would be thrown into the stormy waves. Jesus did not have a boat of his own, but he knew that he could save his friends.

Jesus began to walk on top of the water toward the disciples' boat. He walked straight across the choppy waters, as if he were walking on flat ground. He did not want the disciples to be scared at the sight of him. He reached out to them as he got closer to the boat.

Through the stormy weather, the disciples saw a figure walking toward them. The figure that they saw was moving on top of the water. The figure did not sink, but instead walked right over the waves. Many of the disciples were frightened to see a figure walking on water.

"How do we know that this isn't a trick?" asked Peter. "Maybe it is a ghost that looks like Jesus."

"Jesus wouldn't allow a ghost to take his image and frighten us," said Matthew.

Peter was still scared. He called out to Jesus and asked him to prove that he was real, not a ghost who walked on water.

Jesus could see that Peter was afraid. He looked at Peter and smiled.

Peter said, "Jesus, if it is really you, allow me to walk on water to meet you!"

"Come to me!" he called out to Peter.

Peter climbed out of the boat. He shivered as the cold water hit the bottoms of his feet. Then he stood. Peter walked on top of the water!

Soon, however, Peter began to become afraid. He did not believe what was happening. Peter began to sink. "Lord! Save me!" cried Peter.

Jesus took hold of Peter's hand and pulled him safely out of the water. Jesus said, "O you of little faith, why do you doubt me?"

When Jesus and Peter were safely in the boat, the waves and wind calmed down. Peter was ashamed that he did not believe Jesus' miracle.

The disciples believed that Jesus was truly the Son of God. They rode quietly toward shore together. Soon they arrived in the new land called Genesaret.

The Empty Tomb

Retold by Rebecca Grazulis   Illustrated by Peter Fiore

After they finished their supper, Jesus led his disciples to a garden called Gethsemane.

"Sit," said Jesus, as he pointed to a spot. "I'm going to pray. Keep watch over me."

Jesus went a little way from his disciples. Then he fell to his knees and prayed. He knew that the time of his death was nearing.

Jesus turned to look at the disciples and saw that they were sleeping. "Can you not keep watch with me for one hour?" asked Jesus.

Then Jesus went to pray for a second time.

"Father," he began. "If I must die, let your will be done."

Jesus turned around and found the disciples asleep again. Jesus prayed again. Finally, he woke the disciples.

"The hour has come when I will be given into the hands of sinners. See, the one who betrays me is here!" Jesus said.

At that moment, Judas, one of the disciples, marched into the garden. He was followed by a crowd of angry people and soldiers who carried spears.

"The man I kiss is Jesus," Judas told the crowd. "When I kiss him, take him as your prisoner." Then Judas leaned over and kissed Jesus.

The Roman officers grabbed Jesus and arrested him. Then they took him to Pontius Pilate, who was the governor.

"What has this man done wrong?" asked Pilate.

"He must have done wrong, or we wouldn't have arrested him," the crowd said.

"Then judge him yourselves," said Pilate firmly. "I cannot."

But the crowd continued to argue. They knew that they needed Pilate's order to put a man to death. Finally Pilate agreed to question Jesus.

"Are you the King of the Jews?" asked Pilate.

"My kingdom is not on this earth," Jesus said. "That is why I was born and why I have come into the world—to speak the truth."

At this, Pilate went out again to the crowd.

"I find no guilt with this man," he said. "I need to release someone during the Passover. Do you want me to release Jesus?"

There was a great roar from the crowd.

"No!" they cried. "Crucify him!"

Pilate tried to release Jesus, but the crowd would not have it. They called out, "If you release Jesus, you're no friend of our ruler, Caesar. Everyone who makes himself out to be a king is against Caesar."

Pilate thought the crowd was wrong. "I wash my hands of this," he said.

Still, Pilate ordered Jesus to be crucified. The soldiers wove a crown of sharp thorns and placed it on Jesus' head.

"Hail, King of the Jews!" they called, as they hit him in the face.

The crowd then made Jesus carry the heavy cross on which he would be crucified down the streets of Galilee. Finally they arrived in Golgotha, which means Place of a Skull. There the soldiers hung Jesus on his cross.

There was a criminal hanging upon a cross to Jesus' right and one to his left.

Pilate wrote a message on the top of the cross: "Jesus of Nazareth, King of the Jews."

The crowd shouted at Jesus as he hung on the cross. "If you are the Son of God, save yourself!" they cried.

Others cried out, "Let him put his trust in God now!"

"If you can save others, why can't you save yourself?" another asked.

"Father, forgive them," Jesus prayed.

Jesus' mother, Mary, his mother's sister, and Mary Magdalene stood at the foot of the cross, heartbroken.

When Jesus saw his mother, he called to her, "Behold your son!"

At noon, a heavy darkness covered the entire land. Later, at three o'clock that same afternoon, Jesus called out to his father, "My God, my God, why have you forsaken me?"

Then Jesus said, "I am thirsty."

A man soaked a sponge in a jar of vinegar. Then he attached the sponge to a stick. He brought the sponge up to Jesus' mouth.

After Jesus had finished drinking the vinegar he said, "It is finished!"

Then Jesus bowed his head and gave up his spirit.

Suddenly, the earth began to shake and rocks split in two. The crowd was frightened by the earthquake.

One man said, "Truly, this was the Son of God!"

Soon one of Jesus' disciples, Joseph of Arimathea, asked Pilate if he could take the body of Jesus.

Eager to help in any way he could, Pilate agreed. Joseph wrapped Jesus' body in linen and anointed it with spices, as was the Jewish tradition.

Joseph of Arimathea placed Jesus' body in a tomb and rolled a large stone in front of the entrance.

Three days later, Mary Magdalene visited the tomb. When she got there she saw that the stone had been rolled away. She ran to Simon Peter and told him.

Simon Peter ran to Jesus' tomb. He stepped inside the tomb and saw that Jesus' body was gone. Only his linen wrappings remained.

Simon Peter left, but Mary Magdalene stood outside the tomb weeping. Soon she crept into the tomb and saw two angels in white sitting where Jesus had been.

"Mary," the angels said, "why are you crying?"

"Because they have taken away my Lord and I do not know where he is," she replied tearfully.

After she said this, Mary turned around and saw Jesus. But she did not realize it was Jesus.

"Why are you weeping?" asked Jesus kindly.

Mary thought that Jesus was the gardener, so she said to him, "Sir, if you have taken the body of Jesus, please tell me where you have put him."

"Mary!" Jesus called.

Suddenly Mary knew that it was Jesus.

"Teacher!" she exclaimed joyfully.

Mary Magdalene ran to tell the disciples the good news. And soon Jesus appeared to the disciples himself.

"Peace be with you," he greeted them.

Then Jesus showed them his hands and his side, so that they would believe he had risen from the dead. The disciples rejoiced when they saw Jesus.

Again Jesus said, "Peace be with you." Then he added, "As my father has sent me, I also send you."

Now Thomas, one of the disciples, was not there when Jesus came. "I shall not believe it until I see Jesus myself!" Thomas said.

Eight days later, Jesus came to see the disciples when Thomas was with them.

"My Lord and my God!" exclaimed Thomas.

"You believe because you have seen me," replied Jesus. "Blessed are they who don't see, but believe."

Then Jesus explained to the disciples how they would serve God on earth.

"Go and teach all the nations the ways of the Father, the Son, and the Holy Spirit," he explained. "And remember, I am always with you, even to the end of time."

The End